ESSENTIAL DK COMPUTERS

LINUX
AN INTRODUCTION

BRIAN COOPER

**LONDON, NEW YORK, MUNICH,
MELBOURNE, DELHI**

SENIOR EDITOR Amy Corzine
SENIOR ART EDITOR Sarah Cowley
DTP DESIGNER Julian Dams
PRODUCTION CONTROLLER Michelle Thomas

MANAGING EDITOR Adèle Hayward
SENIOR MANAGING ART EDITOR Nigel Duffield

Produced for Dorling Kindersley Limited by
Design Revolution Limited, Queens Park Villa,
30 West Drive, Brighton, East Sussex BN2 2GE
EDITORIAL DIRECTOR Ian Whitelaw
SENIOR DESIGNER Andrew Easton
PROJECT EDITOR John Watson
DESIGNER Paul Bowler

First published in Great Britain in 2001 by
Dorling Kindersley Limited,
80 Strand, London WC2R 0RL

A Penguin Company

2 4 6 8 10 9 7 5 3 1

A CIP catalogue record for this book is available from the British Library.

ISBN 0-7513-3582-7

Colour reproduced by Colourscan, Singapore
Printed and bound in Italy by Graphicom

For our complete catalogue visit
www.dk.com

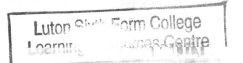

ESSENTIAL **DK** COMPUTERS

LINUX
AN INTRODUCTION

ABOUT THIS BOOK

Linux: An Introduction is for people who feel confident about handling Microsoft's Windows operating systems, and who would like to know about the most credible PC alternative.

I T IS OFTEN SAID THAT WINDOWS IS A well-designed computer desktop, which is let down by the operating system behind it. Linux®, an operating system based on UNIX® and designed by its Finnish creator Linus Torvalds, is now considered as a serious alternative to Windows. This introduction to Linux begins by explaining what it is, and describes some of the pros and cons of using Linux. The operating system's jargon is explained in this book including the word "distribution" – which means the version of Linux being used. The distribution used here is made available by Red Hat®. There is a tour of a Linux desktop, in this case, the GNOME desktop. The remainder of the book looks at programs, file management, customizing, getting online, and finally, installing software.

The chapters and the subsections present the information in the book by using

examples, which in almost every instance are accompanied by an illustration showing how they would appear on-screen.

The book contains several features to help you understand both what is happening and what you need to do.

Command keys, such as ENTER and CTRL, are shown in these rectangles: Enter↵ and Ctrl, so that there's no confusion, for example, over whether you should press that key or type the letters "ctrl."

Cross-references are shown in the text as left- or right-hand page icons: ◻ and ◻. The page number and the reference are shown at the foot of the page.

As well as the step-by-step sections, there are boxes that explain particular features in detail, and tip boxes that provide alternative methods. Finally, at the back, you will find a glossary of common terms and a comprehensive index.

CONTENTS

6   A LINUX INTRODUCTION

14   LINUX DISTRIBUTIONS

20   THE GNOME DESKTOP

40   THE FILE MANAGER

48   SYSTEM CUSTOMIZING

56   ONLINE WITH LINUX

64   INSTALLING SOFTWARE

GLOSSARY 70 • INDEX 71 • ACKNOWLEDGMENTS 72

A LINUX INTRODUCTION

Learning a new operating system is different from learning a new piece of software, which will use many recognizable terms and procedures. This familiarity does not apply to an OS.

WHAT IS LINUX?

Twenty years ago, Linux was an operating system for programmers and computer hobbyists. Today, PCs are sold with Linux preinstalled, and bookshops and PC magazines have sections devoted to it. Linux is now mainstream.

THE FREE OPERATING SYSTEM

Linux is a clone of the UNIX operating system. UNIX is commonly regarded as one of the most powerful and versatile operating systems available, and is widely used as the operating system for computer networks running on large and powerful computers. In the late 1980s, a student at the University of Helsinki, named Linus Torvalds, began to develop a version of UNIX for the standalone workstation – the regular PC that most of us use at home. Since its release in 1991, the original version of Linux has been constantly modified and improved – both by him and a large number of developers who help maintain and update new releases of the kernel ⬑ (the core of the operating system) on a regular basis. Every new version of Linux is made available free-of-charge on the internet for anyone to download. Although this "official" version is regularly updated, anyone is free to make changes to the kernel without fear of litigation because Linux is "open source" software.

WIDENING THE PLATFORM

Linux has now been rewritten and made available for many other operating systems. This means that Linux is now capable of running on many different hardware platforms – from IBM-compatible PCs and Macs to Amigas and Alphas.

Pronounced Linn-ux
Linux is a combination of the originator's name, Linus, with UNIX. It is pronounced Linn-ux with a short "i."

WHAT IS LINUX? • 7

FREE FOR THE TAKING

● You can download and install a fully working copy of Linux on your PC perfectly legally from many sources and free of charge – except for any ISP connection charges that you may pay.

● The reason for this is because Linux is distributed as open source software, with the intention of making it available via the internet for anyone to copy and to modify.

*This Cambridge University website, **www-stud.robinson. cam.ac.uk**, contains useful websites and advice concerning Linux.*

WHAT IS OPEN SOURCE?

● Open source means that the original code, written in a programming language that anyone with knowledge of the language can read, and known as the *source code*, is available to anyone. This means that the code can be examined and altered by anyone. However, open source does not mean the same as "free." There are strict conditions attached to the software, which are specified in its license ▢.

*Internet.com provides a storehouse of Linux applications and documentation at **www.internet.com/sections/linux.html**.*

GNU General Public License
9

REWORKING THE CODE

● The Linux operating system (and much of the software that has been written to be run under it) is supplied to us, the users, complete with its source code. This means that anyone with the skill, time, or inclination to tweak or rework this code can do so.

● Changing source code is strictly forbidden for most if not all the commercial software that you have bought and installed on your computer.

```
int send_sig(unsigned long sig, struct task_struct * p, int priv)
{
        if (!p || sig > 32)
                return -EINVAL;
        if (!priv && ((sig != SIGCONT) || (current->session != p->session)) &&
            (current->euid ^ p->euid) && (current->euid ^ p->uid) &&
            (current->uid ^ p->euid) && (current->uid ^ p->uid) &&
            !suser())
                return -EPERM;
        if (!sig)
                return 0;
        /*
         * Forget it if the process is already zombie'd.
         */
```

The Linux kernel consists of code, such as the example shown here, which you can rework if you wish to.

THE LINUX COMMUNITY

● The freedom to copy and customize is one of the most popular aspects of Linux. For those who like to tweak, or those involved in software development, Linux offers enormous potential. There is also a large online Linux community that shares its knowledge freely.

● The operating system and related software is updated regularly, but if something doesn't work there are many places to seek a fix in addition to the single "official" outlet of the software's manufacturer.

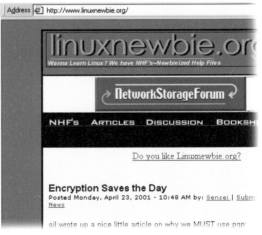

*This site, **www.linuxnewbie.org**, is typical of the many helpful sites that comprise the Linux community.*

GNU GENERAL PUBLIC LICENSE

● Linus Torvalds owns the Linux trademark, but the kernel is distributed under the GNU General Public License. This document has been written by the Free Software Foundation and prevents anyone from restricting the use of any software to which it applies. You can charge a fee or give away such licensed software, but you cannot prevent anyone else from giving it away. Another very important condition of the license is that you are obliged to include the source code.

● The opening text of the document reads "Everyone is permitted to copy and distribute verbatim copies of this license document, but changing it is not allowed."

● The preamble points out that most licenses deprive you of your freedom to share and change the software, but that this license is designed to guarantee that the software is free and that it can be altered and added to by anyone.

GNU General Public License

Linux is written and distributed under the GNU General Public License which code is freely-distributed and available to the general public.

GNU GENERAL PUBLIC LICENSE
Version 2, June 1991

Copyright (C) 1989, 1991 Free Software Foundation, Inc.
675 Mass Ave, Cambridge, MA 02139, USA
Everyone is permitted to copy and distribute verbatim copies of this license do
it is not allowed.

Preamble

The licenses for most software are designed to take away your freedom to sha
contrast, the GNU General Public License is intended to guarantee your freed
change free software--to make sure the software is free for all its users. This G
applies to most of the Free Software Foundation's software and to any other p
authors commit to using it. (Some other Free Software Foundation software is
Library General Public License instead.) You can apply it to your programs, to

Copies of the GNU General Public License are available on many sites including here at www.linux.org/info/gnu.html.

GNU's Not Uni

[Catalan | Chinese | Danish | Dutch | English | French | German | Hungarian | | Swedish | Turkish]

Welcome to the GNU Project web server, **www.gnu.org**. The GNU complete Unix-like operating system which is free software: the GNU s "GNU's Not Unix"; it is pronounced "guh-NEW".) Variants of the GN Linux, are now widely used; though these systems are often referred to called GNU/Linux systems.

- What we provide
- Why we exist
- Where we are going

- How you can hel
- Who we are
- What users think

The principles of the GNU Project are stated on its website at www.gnu.org.

WHY TRY LINUX?

Defining the pros and cons of Linux depends on a number of variables. What kind of hardware will you be running Linux on? What peripherals, such as printer, modem, and monitor, will you be using? What software applications do you intend to run under Linux? Will you be running your distribution of Linux on a network or using it on a standalone workstation? How experienced a PC user are you? However, the following points apply generally to the use of Linux.

THE PROS

MULTITASKING
Linux will run a large number of programs concurrently.

MULTIUSER
Linux can support multiple users concurrently, which is very important for networks, or non-concurrently. This means that multiple users can log in to the same computer and use it as though it were exclusively her/his own computer. Access to each individual's files is password-protected and all other users' files are invisible.

SECURITY
Linux is highly regarded for its security features. Only the system administrator is allowed to make system-level changes, such as installing and uninstalling software, or making changes to individuals' access privileges. It is also claimed that Linux is virus-free.

FREE AND OPEN SOURCE
Linux is open source software 🗋 and free of charge. One huge advantage of open source software is the speed with which fixes for problems are created and made available, usually online.

MODULAR
Because Linux is based on modules, it can be stripped down from its most sophisticated forms, which require hundreds of megabytes of disk space, to run from just a floppy disk.

SHARING WITH OTHER SYSTEMS
Linux can coexist on the same computer as other operating systems. For example, you can choose to boot either Linux or Microsoft Windows on the same PC.

DEVELOPERS TOOLS
Linux is bundled with a wealth of development tools for programmers. The version of Red Hat Linux featured in this book comes with C, C++, Perl, and Python.

NETWORKING
Linux provides an ideal environment to run web and FTP servers. As Linux is based on the UNIX operating system, its networking capabilities are excellent.

7 What is Open Source?

THE CONS

INSTALLATION PROBLEMS

Most of the initial problems are likely to relate to installing and setting up Linux unless someone else sets it up for you. However, you won't be able to install new applications or make system-level changes unless you are in possession of the administrator's password.

EXPERIENCE REQUIRED

Installing Linux is not for beginners. The supplied installation software is usually very good, but you may hit a problem that requires previous experience of operating systems other than Windows. For example, if you are uneasy about identifying the specification of your monitor or running a command from an on-screen prompt, you may want someone else to install the software. You may even need to seek help from a help line, or an online support group 📑.

NOT ENOUGH UNDER THE HOOD

If your PC is old, slow, and has limited capacity, you will have problems running Linux-based software. With an underspecified PC, you will be very lucky to have a graphical desktop, and commands will take a long time to execute.

PROBLEMS WITH PERIPHERALS

Your peripherals may not work under Linux and it is an unfortunate fact that no matter how long you wait, a solution may never arrive. Most problems involve products designed to run specifically under Windows. The win-modem, for example, uses Windows software to replace certain electronic components within the modem's hardware. Linux does not compensate for these missing components in the same way as Windows, and there is no guarantee that it ever will.

SOFTWARE AVAILABILITY

Due to the non-commercial nature of the world of Linux, some software will not be available for Linux, and there is no firm guarantee that it will become available eventually. For example, at the beginning of 2001, Microsoft's Office suite and Internet Explorer were not available for Linux.

GETTING HELP

When you run into difficulties with Linux, run a search in any search engine for "Linux help." You will find an astonishing amount of useful material on the web. This will include links to bulletin boards and mailing lists where people are asking and answering the kinds of problems you may have on a day-to-day basis. Remember, also, to search for Linux in your newsreader and visit any Linux newsgroups that you come across.

HARDWARE REQUIREMENTS FOR LINUX

While Linux can be run on other types of workstations, such as MACs and Amigas, this book is more suitable for users familiar with Microsoft Windows run on IBM-compatible PCs. We also concentrate on Linux for the standalone computer, leaving aside its considerable capabilities for handling networks. This book is largely intended for the curious beginner with experience of Windows rather than the programmer or experienced network user.

REQUIREMENTS FOR RUNNING LINUX

● You can run Linux on an ancient 386, but you will have to run all your programs and commands from the command prompt. However, to use a Windows-type graphical desktop, you will need at least a fast 486 processor, and preferably a high-end Pentium processor.

● Specifications naturally vary depending on what you intend to run under Linux. Simple word processing and spread-sheet applications will require much less processor power than the serious number-crunching required by most graphics applications and the latest 3-D games. If your needs are very slight, you can even find stripped-down versions of Linux that will load from a single floppy disk.

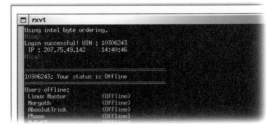

Running Linux on an elderly PC will limit your display to one that resembles the possibly familiar MS-DOS screen.

UFO 2000 is a powerful shoot 'em up game, which has been rewritten to run under Linux.

● For a dual-boot installation of Linux (Linux + Windows), leave plenty of space for the applications you will install later. If, also, you intend to share your computer with others, leave sufficient space for the other users. However, as administrator, only you will be able to install new applications.

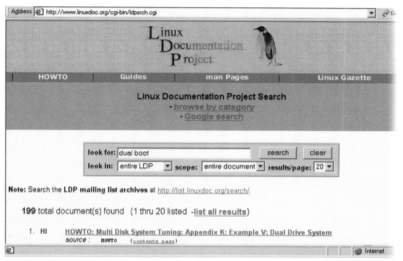

*The Linux Documentation Project at **www.linuxdoc.org** is a site to note. A search for "dual boot" returned 199 hits.*

LINUX INSTALLATIONS

These three specifications would enable the installation of Linux with a graphical Windows-like desktop and a typical combination of utilities and applications.

LOW SPECIFICATION
● 80386, 8 Mb RAM, 540 Mb free hard-disk space.

ACCEPTABLE CONFIGURATION
● Pentium, 32Mb RAM, 850Mb hard-disk space.

RECOMMENDED SETUP
● Pentium processor, 200MHz minimum, at least 32Mb RAM, at least 1500Mb hard-disk space.

ALSO REQUIRED
● CD-ROM drive. Floppy disk-based installers exist, but most distributions occupy at least one CD.
● Supported video card. If you are intending to install Linux on an older PC, you must check whether your hardware is supported by Linux.

LINUX DISTRIBUTIONS

When people refer to Linux, they are generally referring to the bundle of software, code, and documentation that companies such as Debian and Red Hat sell as a "distribution."

WHAT'S ALL THIS JARGON?

Linux can seem heavy on the jargon – especially for beginners – with terms such as X Windows, desktop environments, file managers, X servers, and GUIs. While it is not essential to understand how all the components fit together, it is useful to be familiar with the basic terminology.

Similarly, you don't have to be a mechanic to drive a car, but it helps to know what all the main parts are called, and it is always useful to be able to carry out some routine maintenance. These pages introduce some of the terminology you will encounter when reading about Linux.

THE KERNEL
● At the heart of Linux is the kernel. This is the code that is loaded before anything else when you launch Linux, and is unloaded last when you halt the system. On its own, the kernel doesn't appear to do very much, but without it, nothing gets done. The kernel acts as the main link between your hardware and all the programs that run under Linux. It also handles crucial background tasks such as managing the memory and multitasking.

Next Previous Contents

The Linux Kernel HOWTO

Brian Ward bri@cs.uchicago.edu

v2.5, 28 Mar 2001

This is a detailed guide to kernel configuration, compilation, upgrades, and t

1. Introduction

- 1.1 Read this first! (I mean it)
- 1.2 A word on style

2. Quick Steps - Kernel Compile

Everything about the Linux kernel is in Brian Ward's work at
www.linuxdoc.org/HOWTO/Kernel-HOWTO.html.

THE TOOLS

● Linux tools are a group of programs between the kernel and the software that displays Linux on the desktop. One of the most important tools is the C/C++ compiler. This tool compiles a program written in C or C++, and turns the code into an executable program that can be run by Linux.

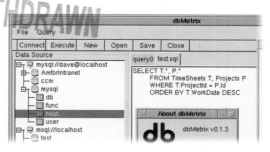

Free tools, libraries, and C/C++ utilities are available at
www.thefreecountry.com/developercity/freelibraries.shtml.

THE APPLICATION SOFTWARE

● In its raw state, Linux does not need a GUI to enable it to work. Here, however, we concentrate on the graphical applications that enable Linux to run as a window-based operating environment.

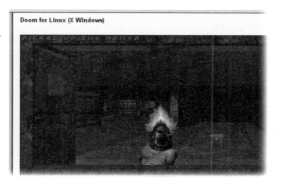

A graphical user interface (GUI) isn't essential, but it's very useful.

X WINDOWS

● The X Window system is used to set up an "X server" on your computer. This holds information about the capabilities of your graphics card and display.

www.softseek.com shows Doom running in X Windows.

WINDOW MANAGERS

● X-based desktop managers provide the graphical interface between your input (via keyboard/ pointing device) and what happens on your monitor. Some window managers look and feel like Microsoft Windows and all are highly customizable. These programs manage the placement of windows including positioning, overlapping, and iconizing.

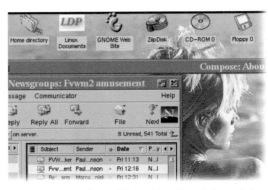

This desktop shows the capabilities of the FVWM desktop window manager. This and other examples are at www.fvwm.org.

DESKTOP ENVIRONMENTS

● The two leading desktop environments are Gnome and KDE. Gnome (GNU Network Object Model Environment), which were developed as open source software.

● KDE (the K Desktop Environment) was built using a GUI toolkit called Qt and is also widely used.

● Both desktop environments are supplied with Red Hat Linux. They are also available with most other popular distributions.

● Certain window managers are incompatible with some desktop environments, but the relevant sites will provide the necessary advice.

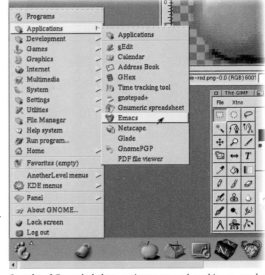

Samples of Gnome's desktop environment, such as this one, can be seen at their website: www.gnome.org.

WHAT DO I GET?

● Your choice of Linux distribution will depend on your assessment of the quality of the vendor's installation program, documentation, and after-sales support.

● The Linux bundle always contains the Linux kernel and a range of the following components:
– Desktop manager
– At least one text editor

– Paint program
– Web browser
– Multimedia tools
– Utilities
– Games
– Programmers' tools

● Many distributions will also provide:
– Technical support
– CDs of third-party applications; full versions of the StarOffice suite are bundled with SuSe and Red Hat Linux
– You will also be supplied with manuals, sometimes running to several thousand pages.

● You can find an up-to-date list of the main Linux distributions, including descriptions and links to the websites of the developers, on the excellent *Linux online* website at **www.linux.org**.

WHERE DO I GET IT?

ON A FREE BOOK OR MAGAZINE CD

● In this form, it's free – if you were going to buy the magazine or book anyway. However, you're not supplied with the distributor's document-ation, and the book is likely to be generic rather than to deal with the specific version you are installing. You also receive little or no commercial software to try out.

DOWNLOAD IT FROM THE INTERNET

● In this form, it's free – provided you are not paying telephone bills and you have a lot of spare time. Downloading Linux, even with only a fraction of the related applications and documentation, can be lengthy. And your online connection must be reliable because you don't want it dropping part way through a download. Also, you must know exactly what you're doing if you decide to download the kernel and build a version of the operating system from this.

BUY IT ON CD

● Some vendors sell a CD containing the bare bones of a distribution, as downloaded from the net, for a couple of dollars. This saves you a lot of possibly expensive and time-consuming downloading. Again, you will have to know what you're doing, and not merely regarding installing the software.

BUY A BOXED SET

● Boxed sets are easy to find. Your software store is likely to sell a boxed set from a main distributor, such as Caldera, Debian, or Red Hat. With this method, everything you need is likely to be provided, including an installation program and printed materials. The only downside is that this method is usually the most expensive.

RED HAT LINUX DELUXE WORKSTATION

The distribution featured in this book is Red Hat Deluxe Workstation, which is not one of the cheaper options available. However, a cheaper version of Red Hat is sold, and all the additional elements can be bought from the same source at a later date. The Deluxe version contains the kind of added software that may be bundled together to form a Linux distribution suitable for professional users.

HISTORY OF EXPANSION

● Red Hat was founded in 1994 as a developer and distributor of open source software. At that time, the number of Linux users was estimated to be 100,000.

● In the intervening period, Red Hat has expanded its activities through acquisitions and software development. Alongside this growth, the number of Linux users is estimated by some to have risen to about 15,000,000.

*The Red Hat website at **www.redhat.com** is the place to start.*

● To see Red Hat's range of products, visit the company's website and click on **Home/Small Business**. You can then scroll down through the page that appears and select **Red Hat Deluxe Workstation** from the list of software.

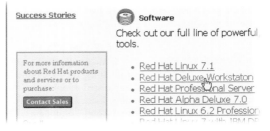

*Scroll down the page and click on **Red Hat Deluxe Workstation**.*

WHAT IT CONTAINS

● Red Hat Linux Deluxe Workstation arrives on 10 CDs, which includes more than 5Gb of a variety of software including:

– Red Hat-tested 2.4 kernel
– GNOME and KDE desktop environments
– Support for USB devices and recordable CD-ROMs
– XFree86 4.0.3, an implementation of the X Windows System
– StarOffice 5.2
– Demo version of Anyware 2.0 that includes the Anyware Desktop, which is an office program suite
– Adobe Acrobat Reader 4.05
– Special Red Hat edition of Yahoo! Messenger
– Game demos from Loki, Alpha Centauri, and SimCity3000
– Over 300 PowerTools applications, including Zope, Gnucash, Openmotif, Exim, FaxMail, and Postfix
– Red Hat Network Software Manager
- Multiple programming languages
– Netscape Navigator.

Red Hat Deluxe Workstation

$79.95 Intel Buy Now or call: US +1 888 REDHAT1

Red Hat Deluxe Workstation is the perfect introdu[...]
for new users. In addition to the award-winning R[...]
operating system, Deluxe Workstation gives you c[...]
guides, office suites, games and services to help y[...]

Red Hat Deluxe Workstation will begin shipping N[...]
23.

Red Hat Deluxe Workstation includes:

Software
● Red Hat Linux 7.1 with source code
● Linux Applications CD Workstation Edition
● PowerTools CD
● Loki CD

Red Hat Network Software Manager
● 60 days subscription for five systems

Support
● 60 days telephone support (two incident limit)
● 60 days web-based support

Documentation
● Installation Guide
● Getting Started Guide
● Documentation CD

| Feature Details |

New features

- Red Hat-tested 2.4 kernel
  Improved support for "hot-pluggable" USB devi[...]
  recordable CD-ROMs.
- Laptop installation class
  Enables PCMCIA support by default.
- Focus on security
  More secure default settings and firewall configu[...]
  installation.
- XFree86 4.0.3 for improved 3D graphics
- Flexible printing configuration tool that supp[...]
  printers
- Introducing Mozilla Web browser.

Demos and applications from partners

- Full version of StarOffice™ 5.2
- Demo version of Anyware® 2.0 from Vista[...]
- Adobe® Acrobat® Reader 4.05
- Special Red Hat edition of Yahoo!® Mess[...]
- Game demos from Loki®: Sid Meier's Alp[...]
  and SimCity®3000

PowerTools applications

- Over 300 applications including Zope, Gnu[...]
  Openmotif, Exim, FaxMail, Postfix and mu[...]

THE GNOME DESKTOP

This section is a quick tour of Red Hat Linux showing the package of features that is installed with GNOME, which is one of the two desktop environments supplied with Red Hat Linux.

LOGGING ON AND OFF

When you start your PC with Linux as the operating system (rather than Windows ME, for example) you will see the screen fill with lines of text that contain information indicating that Linux is checking, enabling, and starting all the software that will drive your system – each followed by **OK** if the check is passed.

ENTER USER NAME AND PASSWORD
● Your exact log-in procedure will have been defined by whoever installed Linux on your computer. If a graphical interface has been chosen, you will see the GNOME log-in screen. If not, you will see a text prompt asking you for your user name and then your password. In either case, supply your user name and password (*not* the root user name and password) when prompted. If you are using a graphical interface, you will usually boot straight into the GNOME desktop environment.

TYPING AT THE PROMPT
● If a graphical interface is not being used, you will see a text prompt similar to this example (where your password replaces **alba**) at the localhost login prompt.
● To start GNOME, type **startx** and press Enter ←.

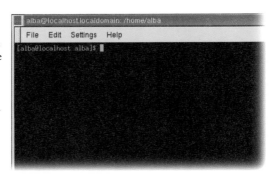

LOGGING OFF

● To log off from
GNOME, choose **Log out**
from the Main GNOME
menu. This displays a
dialog box with up to
three options:
– LOGOUT to end the
GNOME session.
– HALT to shut down
the computer.
– REBOOT to reboot.

USING THE ROOT PASSWORD

If you are a user of a standalone PC, you
may find that Linux places more emphasis
on user names, passwords, and security
than you are used to. If you attempt to
take any action that will make system-level
changes to your PC, you will be required
to enter the root password because the

changes will affect all users of the
computer, not merely you. If you are the
only user of that computer, this may seem
unnecessary. However, if you share your
computer with others, the importance of
limiting these controls to one "superuser"
soon becomes apparent.

THE NEED FOR
THE PASSWORD

● If you do not have access
to the root password –
probably because someone
else has installed Linux –
you will need either to ask
them for the password or
to log in each time that
any system-level changes
are required.

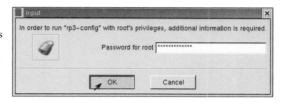

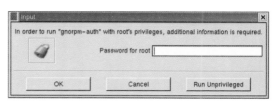

A QUICK TOUR OF GNOME

Once GNOME has loaded, you are presented with a graphical user interface (GUI), which shares many features with other desktop environments, based both on Linux and on other operating systems. Files and directories (folders) are viewed and handled from windows within the

File Manager ⌐. Other drives are accessed through the File Manager itself or via desktop icons. Files, applications, and web pages can also be accessed via icons on the desktop or on the Panel (at the bottom of the desktop). The appearance of the desktop features can easily be customized.

DESKTOP KEY

❶ Symlink to the Home directory ⌐. A symlink is a symbolic link or shortcut that points to a file, directory, or drive.
❷ Trash Icon
❸ Two Red Hat shortcuts
❹ The Dialup Configuration tool ⌐
❺ Symlinks to the floppy disk and CD-ROM drives
❻ Default GNOME desktop
❼ GNOME documentation, available on all subjects
❽ GNOME panel
❾ The File Manager (showing the Home directory)
❿ GNOME panel menus

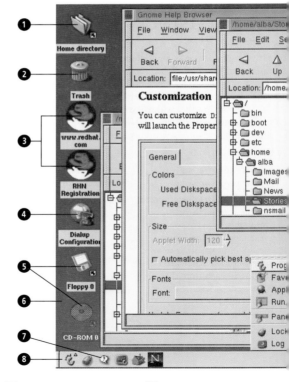

 Using the File Manager 40

Using Symlinks 43

Establishing a Connection 56

UNIQUE APPLICATIONS

At first sight, the Linux desktop may appear to have more similarities than differences with, for example, Windows. However, despite these superficial similarities, Linux has many features unique to itself. It also boasts many unique applets, which are applications and utilities only available with Linux. Most, if not all, of these applications have been written by independent programmers and released under the GNU Public License 🗋. For more information about the authors of these programs, choose **About** from the Help menus of the relevant application.

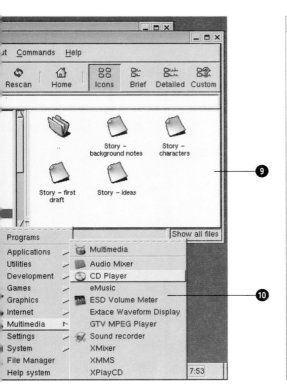

WHICH DESKTOP?

Two desktop environments are provided with the version of Red Hat Linux featured in this book. The illustrations in this book feature GNOME (the GNU Network Object Model Environment), but Red Hat Linux also includes KDE (the K Desktop Environment), which is equally popular and widely used. If you choose to install both desktop environments, it is possible to access KDE programs from the panel while running GNOME, and vice versa. It's worth giving both a try to see which one suits you. They are equally good and your choice will depend only on personal preference.

🗋 **9**   **GNU General Public License**

THE DESK GUIDE

The GNOME desktop and the main groups of software are supplied with a default installation of GNOME.

If you are the kind of user who takes full advantage of a multitasking environment, it doesn't take long for the GNOME desktop to become completely filled with windows. GNOME has an excellent solution for this problem in the form of the Desk Guide, which is a virtual desktop that can hold multiple desktops, each accessible at the click of a button.

DESK GUIDE ICON IN THE GNOME PANEL

● If the Desk Guide feature is already set up on your PC, you will see its icon on the GNOME panel.

● If the Desk Guide icon does not appear there, right-click on the GNOME Panel and choose **Desk Guide** from the **Utility** menu.

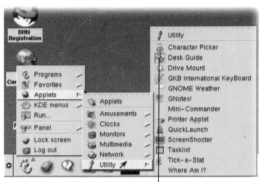

*The **Desk Guide** icon* ●

● In the default four-square Desk Guide, clicking on any of the squares reveals a completely new area of the desktop. Any window you open within any of these windows remains in place until you return to it, thus quadrupling the size of your desktop simply and quickly.

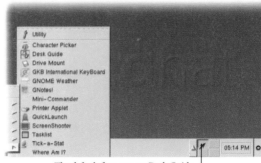

The default four-square Desk Guide ●

CLUTTERED WORKSPACE

● If you are already working with a window and your current workspace is getting too cluttered, click the top-left corner of the window and choose **Send window to Next** (or **Previous**) **Workspace** from the menu that appears. It will immediately be moved to the next workspace.

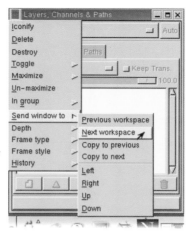

GNOME PANEL FEATURES

● The GNOME panel is the bar that runs along the bottom of the desktop. It is a jumping-off point to applets (mini-applications that work from the panel), and configuration tools that can be customized by the user who can add their own selection of menus and symlinks 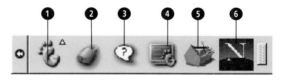 to applications and files. It is also possible to place additional GNOME panels elsewhere on the desktop. The illustration here shows the items supplied with a default installation of the GNOME desktop.

THE GNOME PANEL

❶ The GNOME Button
❷ The Screenlock Button
❸ Integrated Help System
❹ Terminal Emulation Program
❺ GNOME Control Center
❻ Netscape Navigator

43 Using Symlinks

THE GNOME BUTTON

● Click the GNOME button (showing the footprint logo) to display the main menu.

THE SCREENLOCK BUTTON

● Clicking this button opens this panel and locks the screen. It can only be unlocked when the user types their password in the box provided.

INTEGRATED HELP SYSTEM

● This provides comprehensive online help for the GNOME desktop environment.

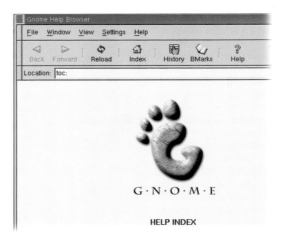

TERMINAL EMULATION PROGRAM

● This enables the user to type commands directly into the Linux operating system.

GNOME CONTROL CENTER

● This enables the user to tweak the applets that determine every aspect of the desktop's appearance and functionality.

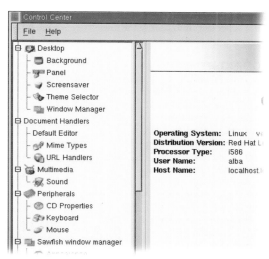

ADDING NEW PANELS

● If you find that the GNOME panel is becoming cluttered, you can create another panel by choosing **Create Panel** from the **Panel** menu. You are given several options regarding the positioning and behavior of the new panel.

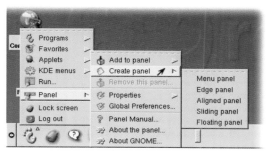

GNOME APPLETS

GNOME applets are mini-applications that are operated from controls that sit in the GNOME panel. The default installation of GNOME with Red Hat Linux includes dozens of useful applets, but it is left to you to choose the ones you would like to place on your GNOME panel. Most of these applets can be customized if you right-click the applet on the panel and choose the appropriate options from the on-screen, pop-up menus.

ADDING ITEMS TO THE PANEL

● To add an applet to the GNOME panel, right-click on a blank part of the panel, choose **Applets** from the pop-up menu and then select the item from the appropriate submenu. You can also choose the Applet menu directly from the main GNOME menu.

● This example shows the CD Player applet being selected and added.

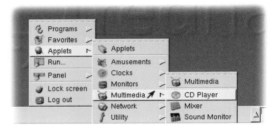

CHARACTER PICKER

● The Character Picker applet enables you to copy and paste special characters, such as accented letters and math symbols, into your document irrespective of the particular application that you are using.

The Character Picker applet ●

AVAILABLE APPLETS

● Six categories of applets are available with the standard installation of GNOME. Among the most useful is Drive Mount, which provides an icon for the floppy disk drive and shows the current state of the drive. Clicking on this icon will mount or unmount the drive. This is quicker than right-clicking and choosing the **mount** or **unmount** menu items, which are the alternatives ⌐.

The Drive Mount applet ●

● WebControl is a simple network applet that enables you to type a web address and go straight to that site. It is available via the **Network** submenu.

● If you are not currently using Netscape Navigator, it will launch the program automatically. If you are running Netscape, WebControl also provides the option to open the website that you have chosen in a new window.

*The **WebControl** menu option* ●

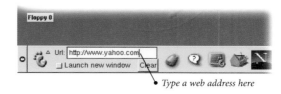

● *Type a web address here*

GNOME PROGRAMS

GNOME (as supplied with Red Hat Linux) includes a very large number and variety of free programs. Grouped under nine main categories, the GNOME programs collection is well worth taking time to explore.

THE PROGRAMS MENU

● If you continue to use Linux, the **Programs** menu is likely to be merely the starting point for using your collection of Linux applications. However, you may find that you continue to use some of these programs, especially as the authors (and other Linux developers) will be regularly improving and enhancing them.

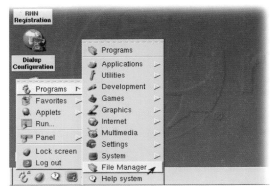

PROGRAMS: APPLICATIONS

● Gnotepad+ and gedit are only two of the text editors available for use with GNOME. They are accessed from the **Applications** submenu of the **Programs** menu.

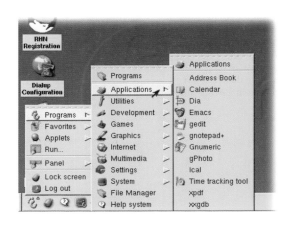

● Gnotepad+ is intended mainly for use as a hypertext markup language (HTML) text editor, with many useful shortcuts for web-page composition.

Gedit is a simple and effective word-processing application.

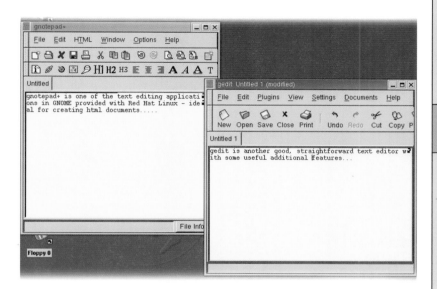

CALENDAR

● The GNOME Calendar is simple, but contains many features you might expect in a commercial product. The Calendar is launched from the **Applications** submenu.

● There are four tabs: **Day**, **Week**, **Month**, and **Year**. Each one displays its own time period, but allows you to schedule appointments from any of the other tabs.

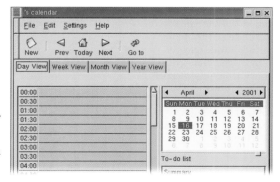

PROGRAMS: APPLICATIONS

● Other applications include Gnumeric, the GNOME spreadsheet, and Dia, a diagram editor. Both of these are very easy to learn – especially if you have some familiarity with these kinds of applications.

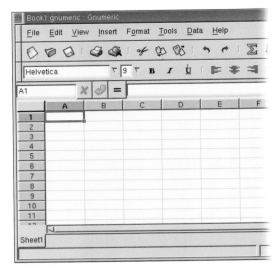

PROGRAMS: UTILITIES

● The utilities accessed from the Programs menu differ from the utilities available as applets because they are full programs that run in separate windows on the desktop. The utilities include a wide range of simple applications, from search tools to calculators to color browsers. The following examples show some of the utilities provided with the standard GNOME installation.

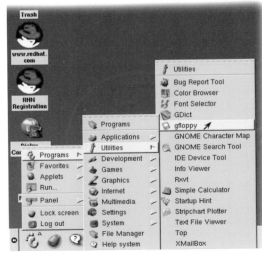

GFLOPPY

● Gfloppy is a utility for formatting floppy disks. You will usually be able to mount and read floppy disks that have been formatted on other operating systems on the GNOME desktop. For example, Windows/DOS-formatted disks can be read. However, the transfer will not work in the opposite direction. Linux floppy disks cannot automatically be read on a Windows PC. So if you are intending to transfer files between a Linux PC (**html** or **txt** documents, for instance) and a Windows PC, you should format your floppy disks as DOS (FAT16) rather than Linux Native (ext 2) disks.

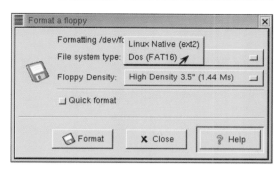

GNOME CALCULATOR

● The **GNOME Calculator** comes with the description as providing "simple double-precision calculations similar to xcalc." For those who require them, there are far more features than the average, free, desktop calculator offers.

PROGRAMS: GRAPHICS

● One of the most highly regarded applications available with GNOME is The GIMP (The GNU Image Manipulation Program). This sophisticated image-editing suite was created as part of a student project in 1995. It is a freely distributed piece of software that is appropriate for image processing tasks, such as photo retouching, image composition, and image creation.

● Before you can use The GIMP, you need to install it on your PC. If you follow the link from the **Graphics** menu, the installation process will begin.

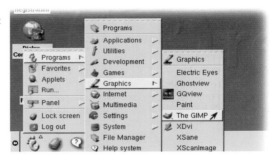

● The installer will lead you though a series of configuration screens until the end of the process has been reached.

● Once installed, you will find that The Gimp has many capabilities. It can be used as a simple paint program, a professional-level photo retouching program, an online batch processing system, an image renderer, and a tool that can be used to convert image formats.

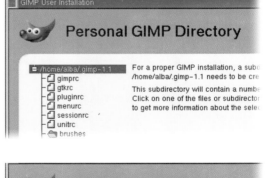

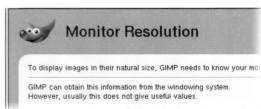

● The GIMP's features include paint tools such as a paintbrush, airbrush, text tools, clone, blur, and sharpen. You can also transform images with rotation, scaling, flipping, and shearing, and save files in many common formats.

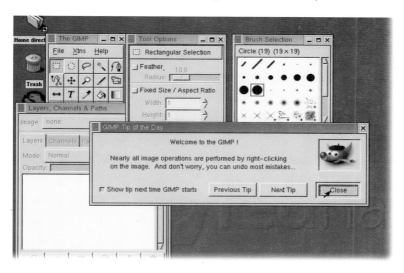

PROGRAMS: INTERNET
● Some of the internet programs listed in the GNOME **Internet** submenu are described later in this book 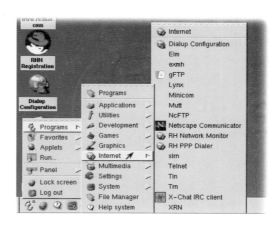.

PROGRAMS: MULTIMEDIA

● To take full advantage of the multimedia programs, you will need to have installed and configured the appropriate hardware (i.e., CD-ROM player, CD-writer, sound card, and sound/video recording equipment).

● The internet is a good source for Linux software for recording, editing, and playing audio and video clips. However, the default applications supplied here provide a good starting point for your collection.

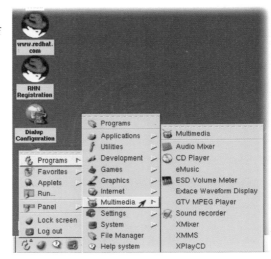

● The GNOME CD Player has all the basic features required of a good, free, desktop, CD player.

● GTV is a simple player for movies that have been recorded in the MPEG format.

A MULTIMEDIA PLAYER

● XMMS stands for X Multimedia System and is a multimedia player for Unix systems, which is more sophisticated than either of the players mentioned. It can play media files such as MP3, MOD, WAV and others.

● The system offers a graphic equalizer, playlist editor, and a wealth of buttons, sliders, and configurable extras.

● Right-click on XMMS and select **Options** to bring up the **Preferences** dialog box.

● The **Preferences** dialog box enables you to install and configure a very wide range of plug-ins relating to audio and visual effects.

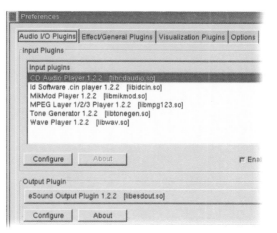

PROGRAMS: SETTINGS

● The **Settings** menu offers many shortcuts to configuration tools, which you can also reach by a number of other routes ⌐.

● Most of the common settings that individual users can change and personalize, such as screen savers, background wallpaper, and system sounds, are accessible via the **Settings** menu.

● This example shows the screensaver settings window that lists and previews the dozens of screensavers available with a standard installation of GNOME. The screensavers can be previewed and customized by clicking the button below the **Screen Saver** selection box and choosing from the available options.

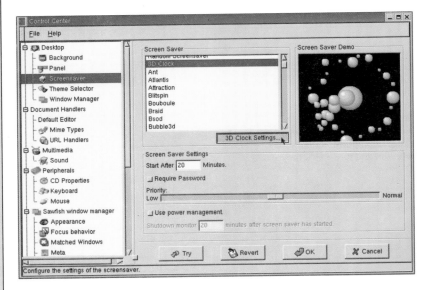

PROGRAMS: SYSTEM

● To use most of the items in the **System** menu, you will need to know the root password because you will be making changes that affect the system rather than simply personalizing your desktop environment.

● Probably the most frequently used menu item here is **GnoRPM**, which is the Package Manager used for installing and uninstalling software in Linux ⌐.

The GnoRPM menu option ●

● Other items here can prove invaluable. The **System Info** option in the above menu opens the **System Information** window, which provides technical information about your computer. You are unlikely to access this often, but it can save you a lot of trouble, especially if you have used the option that enables you to generate a document containing the data and then print it.

● If you should experience difficulties with your PC, you will have the information at hand. To produce this document, start **System Information** from the **System** menu and click on **Save Information to File**.

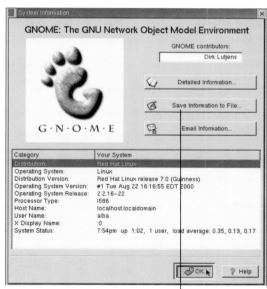

The Save Information to File option ●

The Main RPM Window 64

THE FILE MANAGER

Managing files in GNOME has much in common with the
Windows and Mac environments, but some features will be
more familiar to those with UNIX experience.

USING THE FILE MANAGER

This chapter looks at how to select, move,
copy, and delete files and directories using
the GNOME File Manager. It also looks at

the differences between GNOME and the
Windows and Mac interfaces in accessing
the floppy disk and CD-ROM drives.

WORKING FROM HOME

● When you create and
save a new file as user
rather than superuser (i.e.,
root), by default the file is
placed in a subdirectory of
the **Home directory** named
for your user name. In this
example, the user's name is
alba, so the subdirectory
has the pathname:
/home/alba.

● To open this directory at
any time, double-click on
the **Home directory** icon
on the GNOME desktop.
● To open the **File
Manager** window, choose
File Manager from the
Programs menu on
the GNOME panel.

FILE MANAGER KEY

❶ Left-hand side
The left-hand side of the window displays directories and subdirectories. The contents of the highlighted directory appear in the right-hand side of the window. Click on + to expand the directory tree and - to contract the directory tree in the left-hand side of the File Manager window.

❷ Right-hand side
This side shows the contents of the directory highlighted on the left of the window (i.e., files and subdirectories).

❸ Location box
If you know the pathname (directory/subdirectory), type it here and press [Enter ←] *to open that directory directly in the File Manager window. If you are connected to the internet, you can type an FTP site address in the **Location** box. The File Manager will then become an FTP client application.*

❹ Right Toolbar Buttons
*These four buttons change the view in the right side. For example, **Brief** shows only the file or subdirectory name and no other details.*

❺ Left Toolbar Buttons
These navigation buttons take you to back/forward through directories in a list, or up to a higher directory from a subdirectory.

❻ The Rescan Button
*The **Rescan** button re-displays the contents of the directory currently within the window, reflecting any change to the list of contents that has recently occurred.*

❼ The Home Button
*Clicking the **Home** button changes the active directory to the **Home** directory.*

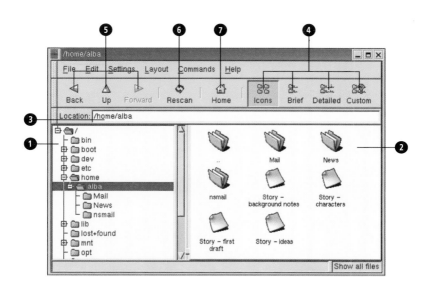

MOVING AND CREATING

When you create or save a file it will be added to your Home directory by default. Most of the file management that you will need to carry out, such as copying, saving, moving, and deleting files, is likely to center on this directory.

CREATING A NEW DIRECTORY
● To create a new directory, right-click in the blank part of the File Manager window and click **New Directory** on the pop-up menu that appears. Then type a name for the new directory in the **Create a new Directory** dialog box and click on **OK**.

MOVING FILES AND DIRECTORIES
● To move files and directories within the File Manager, begin by displaying them in the right-hand panel, highlight those you intend to move and drag them from the right-hand side over to the appropriate directory on the left. When the directory is highlighted, release the mouse button and the files will be moved accordingly.

USING SYMLINKS

In the GNOME desktop environment, a symlink (symbolic link) points to a file or directory that you can either place on your desktop, in a GNOME panel, or in any other folder in the File Manager. The symlink is similar to the shortcut in Windows or the alias in the Apple Mac operating system. You can rename, move, or delete the symlink without affecting the file or directory that it points to.

CREATING A SYMLINK

● To create a symlink, right-click on the file or folder that you want the symbolic link to point to. In this example, the file **Story - ideas** is to have a symlink pointing to it.

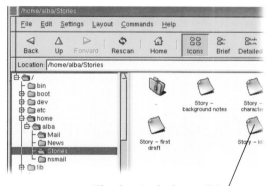

File to be pointed to by a symlink ●

● After choosing **Symlink** from the drop-down menu that appears, the **Symbolic Link** dialog box opens. Type the path and filename for the file in the **Existing filename** text box. In the **Symbolic link filename** text box, enter the name that the symlink is to have. In this example, **Story ideas** is to be a symlink in the same directory as the file called **Story - ideas**.
● Click on OK.

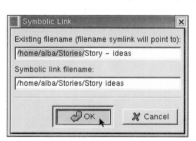

● The symlink appears in the directory window. Double-clicking on this link will now open the main file.

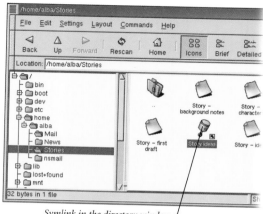

Symlink in the directory window ●

DRAGGING TO THE GNOME PANEL

All aspects of the GNOME desktop environment are highly customizable, as we have seen in earlier pages. If you intend to use any directory on your hard drive regularly, and would like to be able to access it directly from the GNOME

desktop, you can arrange to access it directly from the GNOME panel. Simply drag its icon from the File Manager window over a suitably empty area of the GNOME panel and release the mouse button.

ACCESSING THE CONTENTS DIRECTLY

● To access the directory's contents directly in future, click the icon on the GNOME panel. This example shows the **Home** directory (for the user called **alba**) transferred to the GNOME panel.

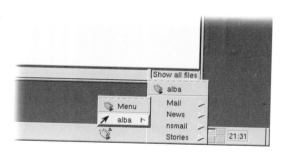

ESSENTIAL KEYBOARD SHORTCUTS

The following keyboard and mouse shortcuts are essential if you are to use the File Manager and GNOME desktop effectively.

Ctrl + DRAG
Hold down the Ctrl key while dragging a file

means that you copy that file (i.e., you move a copy of that file rather than the file itself).

⇧ Shift + CLICK
Use ⇧ Shift + click to select a range of files within the right side of the File Manager window. If you

intend to use this method, it is preferable not to view by icon.

Ctrl + CLICK
To select or deselect a single file from a group, hold down the Ctrl key while clicking on the appropriate file.

THE RIGHT-CLICK POP-UP MENU

Using the right mouse button is one of the most useful shortcuts you can employ in GNOME. When you right-click on a file or an applet, a menu appears offering most of the main options that you will need to use.

– **Open** Opens a file.

– **Open with** Enables you to determine which application to use for opening that particular file, or file-type.

– **Edit** To amend the file.

– **Copy** This produces a dialog box in which you type the new location to which the file is to be copied.

– **Move to trash**

– **Delete** This option completely bypasses the

possibility of retrieving a file, which is offered by first moving an item to the trash can.

– **Move** A dialog box opens in which you enter the new location for the file.

– **Panel** This submenu contains various items including submenus for adding and removing panels and applets.

– **Symlink** This enables you to create a symbolic link, which is broadly equivalent to a shortcut in the Windows or an Alias on the Mac operating systems.

– **Properties** The Properties dialog box contains three tabs, each opening a page containing statistics, options, and permissions, which relate to who is able to edit, copy, or delete the file.

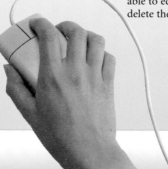

ACCESSING OTHER DRIVES

Linux shows all the directories in one directory tree, irrespective of what drives they are found on. There are no drive letters in Linux; the contents of all disks simply appear as subdirectories. Also, the content of removable disks does not appear automatically; the drives first have to be "mounted" to view their contents.

THE DISK ICONS

● The icons representing the floppy disk and CD-ROM disc drive appear in the lower left-hand corner of the desktop. These icons are symbolic links to the directories **mnt/floppy** and **mnt/cdrom** respectively.

Floppy disk drive icon ●

● *CD-ROM drive icon*

MOUNTING THE FLOPPY DISK DRIVE

● Before you can view the contents of a floppy disk after inserting it into the appropriate drive, you need to mount the drive. Do this by right-clicking the relevant drive icon on the desktop and choosing **Mount device** from the pop-up menu.

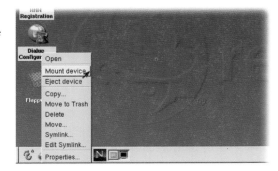

UNMOUNTING A DISK DRIVE

● When you remove the floppy disk and insert another, you will not immediately see the contents of the new floppy disk. With other operating systems, you usually have to use a command to rescan the contents of the disk drive. With GNOME, however, you always need to select **Unmount device** before removing a floppy disk, and then mount the new disk. If you simply rescan the drive using the appropriate File Manager button without unmounting/mounting, you will only see the contents of the first floppy disk. If you physically remove a disk before you have unmounted it, you risk losing the data on it.

CD-ROM DRIVE

● When you insert a CD-ROM disc in the CD-ROM drive using GNOME, an icon will usually appear on the desktop and the File Manager will launch with the CD-ROM directory open, showing the disc's contents. This example shows the contents of one of the CDs bundled with some versions of Red Hat Linux.

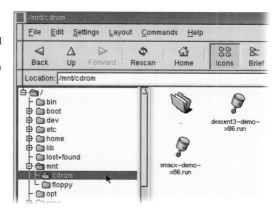

SYSTEM CUSTOMIZING

With the GNOME Control Center you can configure many
aspects of your desktop and your system – from the desktop
background to icons that occupy it.

THE GNOME CONTROL CENTER

Beyond configuring your desktop and
system, you can personalize the smallest
features of the windows and menus that
you work with by using a collection of
tools within Linux, known as "capplets,"
which stands for "Control Center applets."

ACCESSING THE CONTROL CENTER

● Most of the customiz-
ation that you are likely
to carry out is done
through the GNOME
Control Center.

● There are three ways to
access the Control Center:
1 Via the Settings menu.
2 Via the GNOME
configuration tool.
3 Via a GNOME Control
Center option on the
submenu of the Settings
menu. From this submenu
you can access a number of
configuration options.

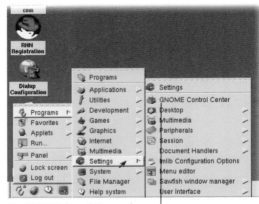

The GNOME Control Center submenu ●

● *GNOME configuration tool*

● The **Control Center** then opens. To access any of the **Control Center** tools, click on the appropriate entry in the left side of the window and the workspace on the right will fill with the relevant controls. If you have used operating systems such as Windows 98 or the Mac OS, you will be reasonably familiar with many of the configuration options you will find in the GNOME **Control Center**.

● The GNOME **Control Center** contains seven main groups of controls:
– Desktop
– Document Handlers
– Multimedia
– Peripherals
– Sawfish Window Manager
– Session
– User Interface

● All these offer submenus, each of which contains many configuration options. Most of these give you the opportunity to test your changes before accepting them as final.

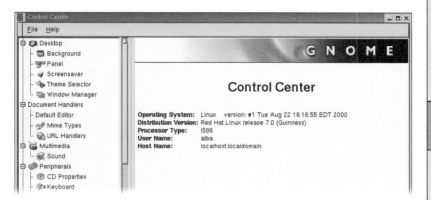

● If you have made some changes without finally accepting them (i.e., you have clicked on the **Try** button rather than **OK**) and you then attempt to quit the **Control Center**, a **Warning** box appears giving you a chance to **Discard all changes**, listing all modules that you have modified.

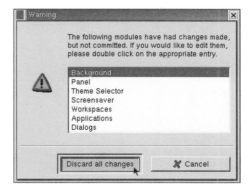

● The next pages show just a few of the dozens of tools, or capplets, that are available via the GNOME **Control Center**, beginning with the area that everyone usually decides to personalize first – the GNOME desktop.

DESKTOP: BACKGROUND

● The tools in the **Control Center** can be used to choose a background from an image file or from a solid color or a gradient. If you choose to opt for a gradient, you need to choose two colors and then specify how these are to be merged.

● Here, as with most other controls, you are given options to try out your changes and revert to the original state if you do not like what you've done.

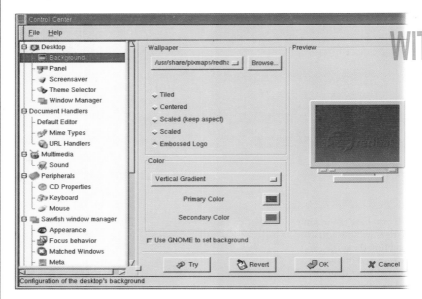

TRY IT FIRST

● To cancel the changes, click on the **Discard all changes** button in the Control Center's **Warning** box. To confirm a change, double-click the highlighted entry in the list and make the modifications. These can then be confirmed by clicking **OK** in the **Options** window.

DESKTOP:
PANEL

● The **Global panel properties** capplet, shown here, gives you options to change almost every aspect of the panel's size, shape, texture, and position.

● This example shows the buttons page. The drop-down menu, that appears when you click the button next to **Button type**, gives you a choice of four button types: **Launcher**, **Drawer**, **Menu**, and **Special**.

● There are four other tabs at the top of the panel window that open pages on **Animation**, **Panel objects**, **Menu**, and **Miscellaneous**. Most of the options that are activated by these buttons and sliders are self-explanatory and you can choose to try, accept or revert by clicking the

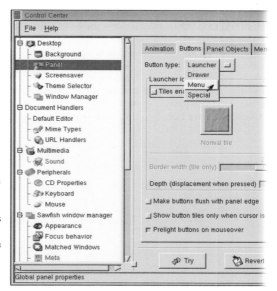

appropriate button at the bottom of the panel window. However, you will not be able to access some

parts of this capplet (e.g., the system part of the Menu page) unless you are logged in as root.

ALTERNATIVE ACCESS

● You can also access the above capplet from the desktop. Begin by right-clicking on the GNOME panel at the foot of the screen, choose **Panel** from the pop-up menu, and then select **Global Preferences** from the **Panel** submenu.

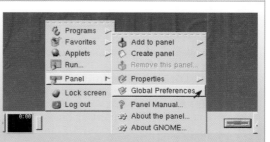

DESKTOP: THEME SELECTOR

● More than a dozen desktop themes are provided with GNOME, and you can preview or select any of them using the **Theme Selector** capplet.

● Clicking the **Try** button will transform the desktop into the theme that you have highlighted in the **Available Themes** box. If you click on the **Preview** button to the right of this box, the theme will only be applied to the material in the **Preview** box below, as shown in this example. If the **Auto Preview** button is depressed, you do not need to click the **Preview** button.

● This capplet also gives you the facility to install new themes, an ever-growing number of which are available on the net.

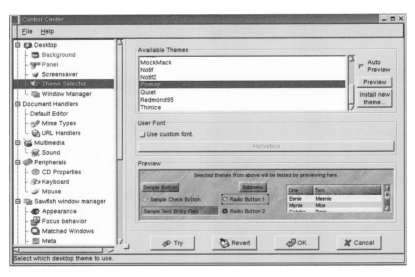

TWO FURTHER CAPPLETS

● **The Session Manager Capplet**
This capplet allows you to control the GNOME Session Management, which specifies the programs that start up, how you save your GNOME configuration, and how you log out.

● **The GNOME Edit Properties Capplet**
With this capplet, you can select which editor will be your default editor while using GNOME. This will allow applications like the GNOME File Manager to launch the correct editor when you try to open files associated with editing. All the popular text editors are included in the selection list.

MULTIMEDIA: SOUND
● You can use the **Sound** capplet to set the sounds for a wide range of GNOME system events.
● First, click the **Sound** Events tab, then highlight an event to which you wish to attach the sound.

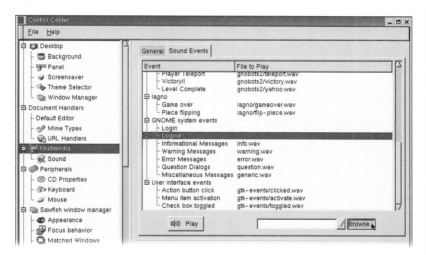

● The **Select sound file** dialog box opens. Choose a sound for the event that you have highlighted, click on the **Browse** button, and navigate to the appropriate **.wav** file on your hard disk. You can preview this sound by clicking on the **Play** button in the **Control Center** window.

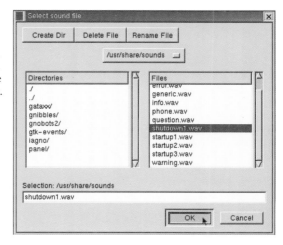

DESKTOP: WINDOW MANAGERS

● You can add window managers by selecting that option in the **Control Center**, and clicking the **Add** button in the top-right corner. In the **Add New Window Manager** dialog box, enter the name, the commands, and the paths required for launching the new window manager with its configuration tool.

● To switch Window Managers, select the required name from the list and click the **Try** button.

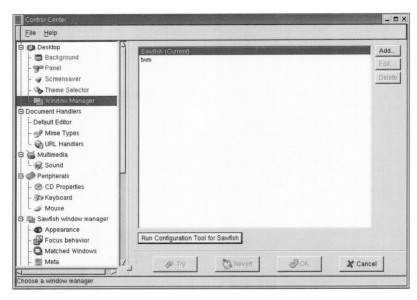

● An **Information** panel tells you that your current session needs to be saved, and how to do it, either now or later.

● You are now switched to the new window manager.

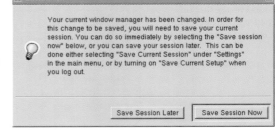

Your current window manager has been changed. In order for this change to be saved, you will need to save your current session. You can do so immediately by selecting the "Save session now" below, or you can save your session later. This can be done either selecting "Save Current Session" under "Settings" in the main menu, or by turning on "Save Current Setup" when you log out.

Save Session Later | Save Session Now

THE USER INTERFACE

● The User Interface (UI) options involve changing the look and feel of applications that are GNOME-compliant. UI options include detachable toolbars and menu bars, and the look of borders, icons, and status bars. The UI capplet is really for advanced users. If you are unsure about any of the options offered here, don't risk making an error that you might later regret.

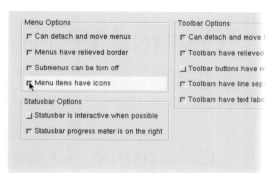

User Interface menu options.

FILE MANAGER PREFERENCES

● One way to access the preferences for the Gnome File Manager is to right-click on the desktop and choose **Desktop Properties** from this pop-up menu that appears on-screen.

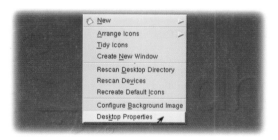

● The **Preferences** dialog box opens. It comprises five tabs: **File Display**, **Confirmation**, **VFS** (Virtual File System), **Caching**, and **Desktop**. The Desktop settings determine the positioning and appearance of text and icons on the desktop.

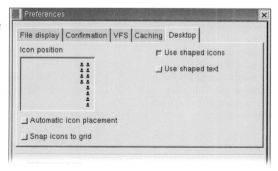

ONLINE WITH LINUX

If you are connecting to the internet using Linux and already have an account with an Internet Service Provider, you will have few problems, provided you know the necessary settings.

ESTABLISHING A CONNECTION

Setting up a new connection means that you will be making changes that affect the way your computer functions. This means that you will be prompted to provide the administrator's (root) password. Without this, you will not be able to proceed.

START THE PROCESS
● The first step in beginning the connection process is to double-click the **Dialup Configuration** icon on the desktop.

ADDING A NEW CONNECTION
● The first **Add New Internet Connection** panel opens. All you should need to do from this point onward is to type the necessary details into each window and dialog box when prompted, and then click on **Next**.

THE KDE ALTERNATIVE

● In the KDE desktop environment, as opposed to GNOME's desktop, the **kppp internet configuration** software is supplied with Red Hat Linux, and provides an alternative to GNOME's Dialup Configuration software.
● Both are equally effective but you can't mix the desktops with the configurations. In other words, if you principally intend to use the GNOME desktop environment, stick with the **Dialup Configuration** tool.

INFORMATION YOU WILL NEED

Be sure to have made a list of the following information before you begin setting up your internet account. This information should be provided by your Internet Service Provider (ISP), particularly if you have previously connected using their proprietary software:
● The ISP's dial-in telephone number (for accessing the internet)
● Your user name
● Your password
● Mail server addresses. There will usually be two of these: one for incoming mail (e.g., **pop3.yourisp .com**) and one for outgoing mail (e.g., **smtp.yourisp.com**)
● Your password for your mail server (a second password is sometimes required by some ISPs to collect your email)
● News server name.

CONFIGURING A MODEM

● If you have a modem attached to your PC (or installed inside it), but it has not been automatically detected and configured during installation of Linux, the **Select Modem** window will open at this point as Red Hat Linux attempts to auto-detect it.

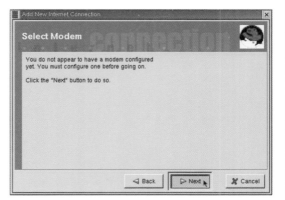

Add New Internet Connection

Select Modem

You do not appear to have a modem configured yet. You must configure one before going on.

Click the "Next" button to do so.

◁ Back   ▷ Next   ✗ Cancel

● Make sure your modem is switched on and connected to the telephone socket. When the modem is found, you are given the options either to adjust the settings or to accept the device as detected. If no modem has been detected, you can attempt to set it up by inputting the settings provided in the modem's manual. In some cases, your modem may not work under Linux 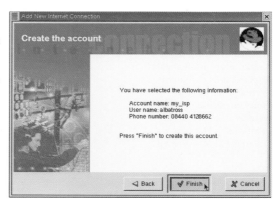.

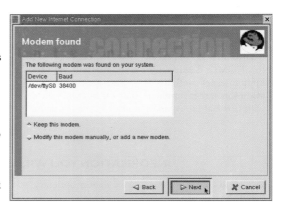

● If you have a fully configured modem, the auto-detect procedure will be unnecessary. After the modem has been confirmed as fully functional, and you have all the necessary information relating to your ISP, the Dialup Configuration procedure should take only a few minutes.

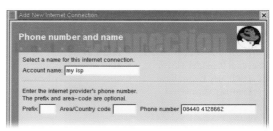

● If you have set up an internet account in the past using Windows 95 (or higher) you will find that the procedure using Dialup Configuration in GNOME is very similar.

11 **Problems with Peripherals**

● Once the procedure is completed, you can click on **Add** to add any accounts with other ISPs you may have. Finally, click on **Close** to complete Dialup Configuration.

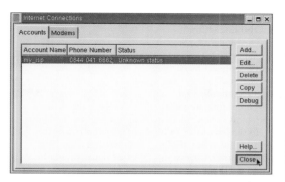

CONNECTING TO THE INTERNET

You can connect to the internet by choosing **RH PPP Dialer** from the GNOME panel. You can place the Modem Lights applet on the GNOME panel for a fast access to an internet on/off button, and a monitor that shows some useful information about the current state of your connection.

PLACING THE APPLET ON THE PANEL

● To place the Modem Lights applet on your GNOME panel, begin by selecting **Panel**, then **Add to panel**, **Applet**, **Network**, and finally choose **RH PPP Dialer**.

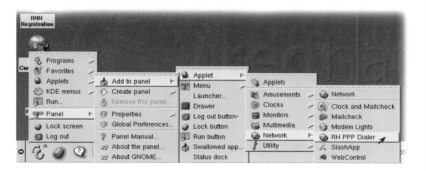

CONTROL YOUR CONNECTION

● The Modem Lights applet lets you connect and disconnect by clicking on the single green light in the center. You can also constantly monitor the status of your modem.

● To the left of the on/off button, the upper display shows data transmission rates; the lower display relates to data received.

The Modem Lights applet ●

● To the right of the on/off button, the higher figure shows the total connection time. The lower figure shows the number of bytes read per second.

● You can customize the applet by right-clicking on it and choosing **Properties** to open the **Settings** dialog box. Here, you can change a number of the applet's settings.

INTERNET APPLICATIONS

● The internet browser that is bundled with Red Hat Linux is Netscape Navigator, which is supplied with the Netscape Communicator suite of programs. At the beginning of 2001, Microsoft's Internet Explorer was not available for Linux.

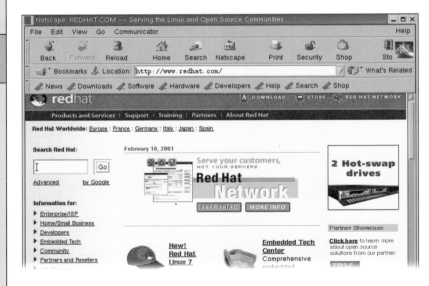

● Netscape Communicator provides an excellent suite of programs including web browser (Navigator), email client (Messenger), Newsgroup client (Newsreader), and the web page editing software (Composer).

● To launch Netscape Navigator, click the Netscape icon on the GNOME panel.

● Netscape Navigator works in Linux as it does in any other operating system. Web page addresses are typed in the Location box and bookmarks can be used to revisit your favorite sites in the internet.

Netscape Communicator icon

MORE INTERNET APPLICATIONS

Red Hat Linux provides a collection of internet programs as part of its standard installation. The number of internet applications available after installing Linux will depend on which distribution of Linux you use. In the case of Red Hat Linux, you will find at least a couple of CDs containing additional programs – many of which will be internet-related. Using your internet connection, you will find an immense number of Linux applications available on the internet.

PROGRAMS VIA THE GNOME PANEL

● The internet programs immediately available with GNOME in this particular version of Red Hat Linux can all be accessed directly from the GNOME panel.

● The small selection here includes various newsreaders, mail clients, Internet Relay Chat clients, Telnet clients, and Lynx, which is a text-based web browser.

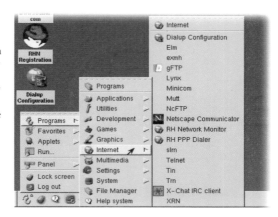

IRC CLIENTS

● Xchat is a no-frills Internet Relay Chat (IRC) client available with the GNOME desktop in Red Hat Linux. Many more feature-laden IRC clients and graphical chat programs are now available for use with Linux than there used to be. A search through the Linux section of software websites, such as **www.tucows.com**, will reveal many examples.

FTP CLIENTS

● FTP (file transfer protocol) clients provide a means of logging on to a remote site from your PC and transferring files to or from that site – provided, of course, that you have the appropriate access privileges required by the site.

● Most anonymous FTP sites simply require your email address for permission to browse and download. This simple FTP client makes the process easy to grasp and execute.

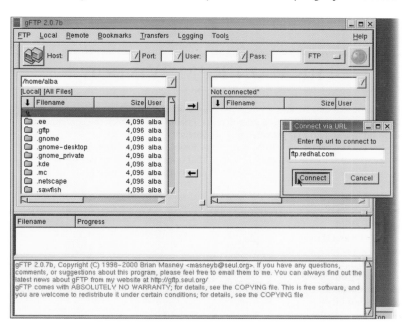

SOFTWARE UNLIMITED

● Virtually limitless Linux software is available on the net. The Tucows software site carries a huge selection of software from every platform you can imagine. The Linux area is regularly updated, well-organized and definitely worth a visit.

● As well as the extensive download library, Tucows also provides a "Head of the Herd" feature, which reviews a piece of leading-edge software. The site also surveys new releases, lists top selections, has a news and editorial section, and provides a help center.

INSTALLING SOFTWARE

Installing software with Linux varies as much as with other operating systems, and depends on how the software has been written and on which installer routine the author has used.

THE MAIN RPM WINDOW

The Gnome Red Hat Package Management system (RPM) is a graphical front-end to a system that provides a software control center. This RPM can:
– Show you all software packages currently on your system
– Enable you to add or delete packages
– Enable you to check the contents and integrity of any package
– Enable you to reinstall any package that does not appear to be functioning correctly.

RUNNING THE GNOME RPM

● It may be useful to think of a "package" as the way in which software is conveniently bundled for ease of installation and access within Linux. Installation often requires files to be installed in several different locations on your PC to function correctly. RPM helps you keep tabs on these files.

● You can run the Gnome RPM from the Gnome Panel (as shown here) or directly from the command line if you prefer working with text-only commands.

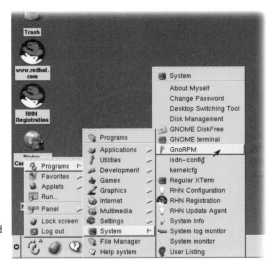

A FILE MANAGER WINDOW

● The Gnome RPM window displays the packages on the computer by arranging them into groups in the left-hand panel under **Packages**.

● In the right-hand panel, the contents of a group highlighted on the left appear as icons. To find out more, or to carry out any actions on a package, click its icon and then click the relevant toolbar button.

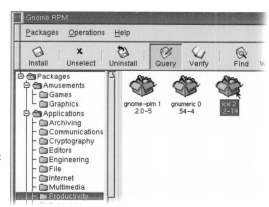

INSTALL AND UNINSTALL BUTTONS

● The **Install** and **Uninstall** buttons add or remove the package from your system. Once a package has been uninstalled, it is removed from the Gnome RPM.

QUERY BUTTON

● Clicking the **Query** button on the toolbar opens a **Package Info** dialog box, which gives information about the selected package.

● In this dialog box, you will find a row of buttons along the bottom that can be used to perform operations, such as install/uninstall or query, on individual packages.

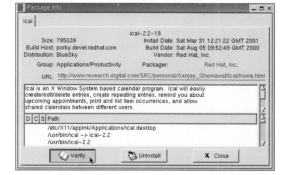

VERIFY BUTTON

● Clicking the **Verify** button in the **Package Info** dialog box checks the integrity of the files that make up a selected package and ensures that none has been tampered with or corrupted.

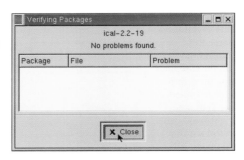

LOCATING WHAT YOU WANT

There are three main sources of software for Red Hat Linux: first, the collection of CD-ROMs supplied with the boxed distribution, second, the CD-ROMs given away with some magazines and books, and third, the libraries on the internet.

SOFTWARE FROM THE DISTRIBUTOR'S CD

● When you insert a CD supplied with the boxed Red Hat distribution, a dialog box asks if you want to auto-mount the CD-ROM. Choose **Yes**, and the **Install** window opens.

● Initially, the packages that are currently installed on your PC are shown. To view the CD's contents you need to click the **Install** button.

● The CD's contents now begin to appear in the **Install** window. To view these contents more easily, click on the **Expand Tree** button.

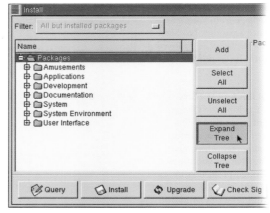

USING THE QUERY BUTTON

● You will make most use of the **Query** button when exploring the contents of a CD. Although the software on the CD is grouped into categories, you will want to know more about a package before installing it on your PC.

● Highlight the files you are interested in, check the boxes next to them, and then click on the **Query** button.

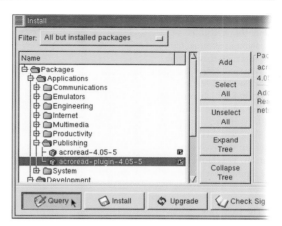

● Information relating to each file appears in a separate panel within the **Package info** panel that opens.

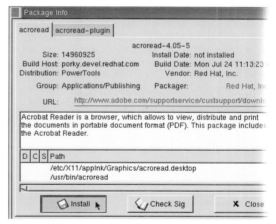

● If you decide to proceed with the installation from the CD, click on the **Install** button. You can follow the progress of the installation in the **Installing** window.

SOFTWARE FROM THE INTERNET

● If you are connected to the internet, the Gnome RPM offers a very useful net download feature, **Rpmfind**, which you can access from the main RPM window.

● To access this facility, click on the **Web Find** button. This launches the **Rpmfind** window.

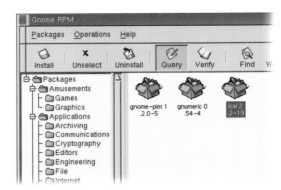

● The first time you use the **Rpmfind** window, you are connected to an FTP site that holds the RPMfind database. This downloads a list of packages that appear in the left hand panel under **Name** and **Distribution**. Each time

you click a plus sign to reveal a submenu, more information is downloaded from the database. In this way, you can access every package that is contained in the database.

● To search the database, type a search term in the

box at the top of the window and click the **Search** button. A list of hits appears in the left-hand panel. You can treat these as any other packages within RPM by clicking any entry, followed by the **Query** button to find out more.

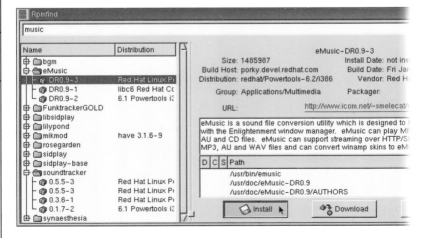

DOWNLOADING THE SOFTWARE

● When you click on **Install**, the package is installed onto your PC, and it becomes accessible through the RPM in the same way as all the other packages on your PC.

WHERE HAS MY SOFTWARE GONE?

This isn't quite such a naive question as it might sound. Newly installed software does not necessarily always install symlinks (shortcuts, as Windows calls them) in the Gnome panel. This means that, once having installed a package, you may find yourself not completely sure about how to launch the program.

COMPLETING THE INSTALLATION

● In the example shown here, the internet application called **Payment Client 2.1** does not fully auto-install. This is typical of many packages in that it requires some action by you before it is fully configured and ready to use.

● To find out what to do next, you need to locate the **Read me** file, which you will usually find in an appropriately named directory within the **usrs-doc** directory on your hard drive. In this case, it reveals that some simple, post-installation configuration is required by the user. This is far from being unusual with package installations.

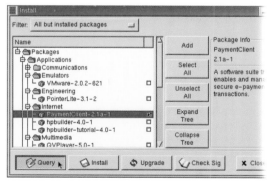

GLOSSARY

C The name of a programming language designed during the early 1970s and used to reimplement Unix.

CLIENT The client is the program, or end of a system, which is receiving the service being provided.

COMPILE To turn a program from source code into an executable machine code file, which cannot be read by any human.

DEBIAN A free, open source, operating system for a computer that uses the Linux kernel.

DISTRIBUTION A combination of a Linux kernel, a suite of command programs, and other software for installing and maintaining a Linux system.

DRIVER Computer code that translates device-independent instructions into commands that a real device, such as a disk drive or a printer, can understand.

GIMP The "GNU Image Manipulation Program" is free software suitable for manipulating images.

GNOME A desktop manager providing a range of tools to support window managers.

GNU "GNU is Not Unix" refers to the GNU operating system begun by the Free Software Foundation to create a free operating system.

GRAPHICAL USER INTERFACE (GUI) Allows the user to interact with a computer system in a visual manner with a minimum of typing.

HOME DIRECTORY A directory provided to store the personal files and directories of a user.

HTML "Hypertext Markup Language" is the form in which web documents are transmitted and interpreted by browsers.

ISP "Internet Service Provider" is an organization that provides people with networked access to the internet.

IRC "Internet Relay Chat" is a worldwide, online "party line" network that allows conversations to take place in real time.

KDE A project to make Linux more user-friendly by providing a GUI interface, or desktop, between the user and Linux.

KERNEL The core of an operating system that contains the most primitive functions on which more sophisticated functions depend.

MODULE A piece of the kernel that performs a specific task.

MS-DOS The "Microsoft Disk Operating System" installed by IBM on their first personal computers.

MOUNT This command allows the contents of a disk to be placed in a subdirectory of a file system.

OPEN SOURCE Software for which the source code is freely available, to be used, changed, and redistributed.

OPERATING SYSTEM The essential software of a computer that schedules tasks, allocates storage, and provides an interface between the user and applications.

PPP "Point-to-point protocol," is the most popular way of connecting a computer to the internet via a dialup modem.

ROOT The specially privileged account on a computer system that has absolute control over it.

SOURCE CODE The readable text that programmers create. Source code is compiled for computers to use and is then unreadable. Source code for non-free software is kept secret while the source code for free software is always available for anyone to fix or improve.

URL "Uniform Resource Locator" is an address that identifies a document or computer on the world wide web.

WINDOW MANAGER A program that manages a graphical user interface by determining the appearance of windows and the response to input by the user.

X WINDOWS This graphical user interface manages all screen activity and is accessed by programs to provide their display requirements.

INDEX

ABC

advantages of Linux 10
aliases *see* symlinks
applets 23, 28–9
  see also capplets
application software 7, 15
availability 6–7
  distributions 17
  software 11, 62, 66–9
calculator 33
calendar 31
capplets 48–55
  see also applets
CD-ROM drive 47
Character Picker 28
chat programs 62
configuration
  modem 57–8
  requirements 12–13
  software 69
connection, internet 56–61
Control Center 27, 48–55
customizing 48–55

DEF

Desk Guide 24–5
desktop environments 16
  see also GNOME
development tools 10
dialup configuration 56–9
directories 40–2
distributions 14–19
documentation 7, 13, 14
downloading software 17,
  68–9
drives 29, 46–7
dual-boot installation 10, 13
File Manager 40–7, 55
File Transfer Protocol (FTP)
  63
files 40–4
fixes 10
floppy disks 33, 46
FTP *see* File Transfer
  Protocol

G

Gimp, The 34–5
GNOME 16, 20–39
  applets 23, 28–9
  Control Center 48–55
  customizing 48–55
  Desk Guide 24–5
  desktop 22–7, 50–3
  File Manager 40–7
  GNOME panel 22, 25–7,
    28, 44–5, 51
  logging on/off 20–1
  programs 30–9
  RPM 64–6
GNU General Public License 9
graphical user interface
  (GUI) 15
graphics programs 32, 34–5
GUI *see* graphical user
  interface

H

hardware requirements
  12–13
help 8, 11, 26

IJK

icons 22
installation 11, 64–9
internet 8, 17
  connection 56–61
  programs 35, 61–3
  software download 68–9
Internet Relay Chat (IRC)
  clients 62
KDE (K Desktop Environment)
  16, 23, 57
kernel 14

L

libraries 15
license 7, 9
logging on/off 20

M

modems 11, 57–60
mouse 45

multimedia 36–7, 53
multitasking 10
multiuser 10

NO

Netscape Navigator 29,
  60–1
networking 10
online access 56–63
open source 7, 10

PQ

passwords 20–1, 39
peripherals 11
preferences 55
processor requirements 12–13
programs 30–9, 61–3
  see also software
Query button 65, 67

R

Red Hat 18–19
Red Hat Package
  Management (RPM)
  System 64–6
RH PPP Dialer 59
root password 21, 39
RPM *see* Red Hat Package
  Management System

S

screenlock 26
screensavers 38
security 10
Session Manager 52
settings 38
shortcuts 45
  see also symlinks
software
  applications 7, 15
  Gnome 30–9
  installation 64–9
  sources 11, 62, 66–9
sound *see* multimedia
source code 6–9, 10, 17
spreadsheets 32
support 8, 11

symlinks 22, 43–4, 69
system information 39

T
terminal emulation 27
text editors 30–1

tools 10, 15
U-Z
User Interface 55
utilities 15, 32–3
viruses 10

WebControl 29
window managers 16, 54
Windows, dual installation 13
X Windows 15

ACKNOWLEDGMENTS

PUBLISHER'S ACKNOWLEDGMENTS
Dorling Kindersley would like to thank the following:
Paul Mattock of APM, Brighton, for commissioned photography.
fvwm.org, gimp.org, gnome.org, gnu.org, Christopher Heng, internet.com,
linux.org, linuxdoc.org, linuxnewbie.org, Robinson College, Cambridge,
softseek.com, sourceforge.net, David E. Storey, Brian Ward, xmms.org.

Red Hat Inc. for permission to use screenshots from Red Hat Linux.

Every effort has been made to trace the copyright holders.
The publisher apologizes for any unintentional omissions and would be pleased,
in such cases, to place an acknowledgment in future editions of this book.